I0088027

Organize Your Life NOW!

Easy Steps for Organizing Your Mind & Your Surroundings

JEAN WELLES

Copyright © 2016 Jean Welles
All Rights Reserved.
Published by GraciousPublishing.com
11664 National Blvd. #275, Los Angeles, CA 90064
ISBN: 9781942088011

Contents

Introduction

In the early 1900's, people were speculating that in just a few generations no one would need to work more than 3 hours a day! They witnessed the inventions of all kinds of new technologies.

In fact, John Keynes wrote an essay in 1928 called "Economic Possibilities for Our Grandchildren." In it, he said that no one would need to worry about making money and that people would have more leisure time.

It is true that many new technologies have made aspects of living in the 21st Century easier than a hundred years ago. We have dishwashers, kitchen gadgets, computers, iPads, smartphones, robotic machines to do work, and much more.

But, instead of having more leisure time, people are busier than ever and many feel overwhelmed. Recent polls have shown that over half of the US workforce feels overwhelmed at least some of the time. Have you ever felt overwhelmed? I certainly have!

This book is going to address both how to overcome overwhelm and how to put together a system to unclutter both your mind and your environment.

It is a new era and we can use some of the tools of the 21st Century to help us organize our activities and possessions. This book will map out a plan to help you cut through the clutter and come out the other end with tools to organize your life now.

I remember one day coming home, walking into my workspace, and thinking, "Who made this mess?" Then, it occurred to me, that no one had been in there, but me! As I looked around, it hit me that I was the one that made every pile of clutter. It didn't just happen by itself.

The problem was, I never had a system or a plan. Instead of putting things away, I put them down in a visible place so it would be easy to work on it again. That was a terrible mistake.

If you struggle with clutter, you are going to love this book. There is definitely hope for the worst 'clutterer'. You'll find easy to implement solutions in this book. Plus, you'll discover many new tips on managing your time and priorities.

Besides organizing things, in this book, you'll be encouraged to think about bigger purposes in your life. In these pages, you will find help for organizing both your thoughts and things.

In this book, you will learn why you need to get organized. Then, you'll learn about organizing your thoughts. Yes, our minds can feel cluttered, too. You'll learn tips for clearer thinking.

There are small easy tweaks that you can do which will help you in your goal to becoming more organized and productive. Your thoughts and even how you hold your body can change the chemistry in your brain. There are fascinating studies I think you'll enjoy learning about!

Next, you'll learn some neat strategies for keeping your physical space clean and uncluttered. This can be your work space, but can also apply to other areas like your kitchen, garage, family room, etc.

After looking at being organized inside and out, we'll touch on ideas of how to structure routines in your day. Then, we'll discuss important topics like taking good care of your health. Most diseases can be avoided or reversed with a good diet, exercise, enough sleep, and watching how we think.

I hope this book helps to inspire you to be more organized and free of clutter inside and out. In addition to the ideas here, you can download '50 Clever Organizational Tips' at **GraciousPublishing.com/50tips**.

The beginning of a clutter free life can start today.

Why Get Organized

In this chapter, we're going to look at why it's a good idea to get organized. We'll look at the cost of clutter and the major benefits of having a clutter-free organized space to live and work in.

Let's look at a few of the costs first.

Cost of Clutter

I can tell you from firsthand experience that clutter around your home will drain you. It can make you feel overwhelmed and cause you to waste hours trying to find items, like your keys or glasses.

Clutter can cost you time. It can be especially stressful trying to find important items. Have you ever been late to an appointment because you couldn't find your car keys? Have you lost important items, like checks or invoices?

Clutter can cost you money. It's not uncommon to purchase the same items over and over when you can't find the original. It's a waste of money.

A neighbor of mine told me she is constantly losing her reading glasses. She now buys packages of reading classes from Costco, in anticipation.

If you are self-employed, time spent looking for items is

time not spent on your business. If you work for someone else, looking for items can pull you away from productive time on your job.

Clutter can affect the people around you. When you are stressed trying to find items, it affects everyone else in the household or workplace. It is difficult for others to live around the clutter. It can even be embarrassing to invite people into your cluttered home or office.

One of my friends confided to me that she is so embarrassed with the clutter in her home that she never invites anyone over. She is too embarrassed to have anyone see it.

Money, time, stress, embarrassment, frustration, feeling overwhelmed, and on and on. Clutter is not your friend. Regardless of where you are today, there is hope. Yes, it is possible to learn to organize your space and life.

Having clutter around can be detrimental to your health. Now we'll look at a few benefits of getting your life organized and your environment clutter-free.

Benefits of Being Organized

When you get organized you will be able to focus on achieving your goals. You save time, because you'll know where everything is. Yes, I really do mean you can use a system to put your hands on any document or item you own. Would you like to never misplace your keys again?

Because there are less distractions, it's easier to concentrate. When you are focused, you can be more productive and less stressed. Because you are more productive, you can get more done in a shorter time. In fact, you can get things done, period.

How many projects go uncompleted?

It's very easy to get distracted when there are stacks of papers or other items out. When your home and workspace are clean and organized it is much easier to focus on the task at hand.

Multitasking is not a good idea. When you are laser focused on one item at a time, you can absolutely be more productive. It's been found that people cannot efficiently multi-task. Instead, multitaskers continually shift focus to different tasks. Then, it actually takes longer to complete any of them than it would have by simply focusing on one project at a time.

Can you imagine yourself at a clutter-free desk or walking into a clutter-free home? No need to ever feel embarrassed if a friend just drops by. You can be proud of your home and feel good about having people over.

Can you envision waking up in the morning with a plan that both helps you to get healthier and that uses your talents to enrich other people's lives? We are both social and spiritual beings, and, in the next chapter, we will touch at how to grow stronger in all areas of our lives.

We'll look at more specifics on organizing your surroundings in a later chapter, but now that you can see some of the costs of clutter, why not start today cleaning your desk, your kitchen, or whatever physical area that has clutter.

Set a timer for 10 minutes and just get started. Sometimes when you're feeling overwhelmed just getting started can be hard. Anyone can find 10 minutes.

Action Items

- Find one area in your home or office that is cluttered.
- Set a timer for 10 minutes and see how much you can get done. (I suggest starting with your desk.)
- Focus on one area at a time.

Do you see how easy this is? Do you think you could take 10 minutes a day to organize your space? It's not hard when you think of taking just 10 minutes.

Now that we have looked at some of the reasons why it's important to get organized, let's dive in with a few of the specific techniques and ideas to make it a reality. I'm excited for you in some of the things you'll learn here.

In the next chapter, we'll look at some ideas for organizing your inner life, your thoughts.

Organize Your Thoughts

In the last chapter, we looked at a of few of the reasons why being in an overly cluttered environment costs you time, money, and stress. Naturally, the benefits of being in an uncluttered and organized space are immense.

Are you becoming aware of how it not only helps you to focus but is a joy to see? Have you done the action item at the end of the last chapter? It just takes 10 minutes.

Now, we are going to attempt to tackle organizing your inner life. There is so much information being thrown at us every day. It's easy to feel overwhelmed. But, when you are mentally overwhelmed, it's actually hard to make decisions.

Our inner lives can feel cluttered. Instead of getting up every day and just reacting to whatever happens in the day, you can be proactive and work on your goals. You can even think about how you can impact the lives of the people around you.

In this chapter, we're going to look at the importance of well-rounded Life Goals. Then, in the next chapter, we'll cover something I'll call a Brain Dump.

If you can get all those thoughts in your head on paper or captured into a software program, it's very freeing. Then, we are going to discuss how to actually implement your goals and dreams.

Life Goals

Do you have goals? Life can get busy and we can lose track of some of the most important areas of our lives. Having goals and planning them into your day gives your life focus and helps you to accomplish more with less time.

With clear goals, it helps you to discard the activities that do not line up with your biggest priorities. There was a famous study done with Harvard MBA graduates. In 1979, the new graduates were asked if they had clear, written down goals for their future and had made plans to accomplish them.

Here are the results:

- 84% had no specific goals at all.
- 13% had goals, but they were not committed to paper.
- 3% had clear, written goals and plans to accomplish them.

In 1989, just 10 years later, the interviewers again interviewed the graduates of that class. Can you guess the results?

The 13% of the class who had goals were earning, on average, twice as much as the 84% who had no goals at all.

Even more staggering – the 3% who had clear, written goals were earning, on average, ten times as much as the other 97% put together.

(Source: from the book *What They Don't Teach You in the Harvard Business School*, by Mark McCormack)

We each have just one life. Don't you want to live it to the fullest? These were financial goals, but living just to make a lot of money is not going to bring you true contentment. Your goals should be well-rounded and include all the important areas of your life.

Money alone is not enough. There are so many rich and famous people that have committed suicide. Fame and wealth are by themselves not the means for true happiness. Many in the height of their careers struggled with depression, or drugs and alcohol.

My brother, now a retired children's pastor, told me of a multi-millionaire he knew who confided in him that although he had everything money could buy, in reality, he actually felt very empty inside.

We are social beings and good relationships are important. One of my friends told me about a sweet little Chinese woman married to a Chinese doctor. He left her for a younger woman and shortly after, she committed suicide.

Winnie was so upset. They had no idea that this woman was depressed. She was instrumental in raising money to send the high school orchestra to a competition in Rome.

Winnie said that all this woman needed were a few good girlfriends to support her, and tell her that her husband was a creep. She needed to know that she had great value. This Chinese woman viewed herself solely through her husband's eyes and thought she was worthless.

For me, the most important goal centers around my Christian faith. I believe we were created by a loving God and that He has created each one of us with unique gifts and talents.

When we can tap into why we were created, there is true contentment and real purpose in this life. What do you enjoy doing? What are you good at? Do you have a passion? A keen interest?

Here are a few fun quotes about goals:

First Quote

"You are never too old to set another goal or to dream a new dream."
C. S. Lewis

One of my guitar students, who was a Grandmother at the time, told me that her mother had taught her to stay young by continuing to learn new things. She told me that her mother learned to swim at age 90! I love hearing stories like this.

If you don't use it, you lose it. At a nearby senior center I met Sam, who at age 86 loves to use the outdoor park to do his exercise routine. He is still very flexible and enjoys working out.

On the news last year, I saw the inventor of the plastic bead jump rope, Bobby Hinds. At age 80 he is still inventing new health gadgets, and on the show, jumped rope as well as he did in his 40's!

There are some amazing videos on YouTube of athletes in their 80's and older. For example, Harriette Thompson, age 92, still runs marathons. Sister Madonna Buder, at age 82, is the oldest person to complete an Ironman Triathlon.

An 87 year old gymnast, Johanna Quaas, still competes and can do incredible feats of strength on the parallel bars. She's stronger than many people 1/3rd her age!

In an interview, Johanna says that a secret to her youthfulness was eating a healthy diet with not too much or too little food. She said that she eats a lot of greens. She didn't mention it, but you know she has spent countless hours training her body.

We will all get older, but if you continue exercising, eating right, and taking good care of your body, it is possible to live a high-quality life into your golden years. What you do today will absolutely affect all of your tomorrows. Just look at Johanna still competing in gymnastics at age 87!

It's obviously true that you are never too old to start something new! Look at Grandma Moses who did not start painting until her 70s. Her exhibitions were so popular, they broke attendance records all over the world.

Second Quote

"If you want to reach a goal, you must 'see the reaching' in your own mind before you actually arrive at your goal."
Zig Ziglar

I love Zig's quote about seeing the end result when you are working towards your goals. He loves to say that having a life without goals is like playing a game of basketball without nets. How can you play the game without scoring shots?

Speaking of basketball, another famous study was done with basketball players. Dr. Blaslotto, at the University of Chicago, split people into three groups and tested each group on how many successful free throws they could make.

One group was told to practice free throws for an hour every day. The second group was told to just visualize themselves making perfect free throws without actually touching the basketball. And, the third group was told to do nothing for 30 days,

After 30 days, he tested them again. Here are the results:

- The first group improved by 24%.
- The second group improved by 23% without touching a basketball!!!
- The third group did not improve, which was expected.

In this study, visualizing yielded essentially the same benefit as practicing. This important discovery is that, when we see a successful result, something happens to us. With a clear end result in mind, it's easier to accomplish goals of all kinds.

One of my guitar teacher, David Grimes, told me many years ago that he never performed a piece in concert until he could completely visualize it in his mind. He saw both the music and where to play on the fretboard.

Many top notch musicians do this. These folks can practice their music without their instrument. Beethoven even wrote his last symphony when he was almost completely deaf, the 9th symphony. It's one of his most famous works.

What are your goals? Have you thought about what you would like to achieve and what kind of person you would like to be? Here are some suggested goal areas. These are important to me, but you can certainly make your own list.

Suggested Goals

Here is a list of areas that is a good place to start:

- Spiritual
- Family & Friends
- Health
- Work & Finances

- Service/Community

This is just a suggested list to give you some ideas of types of goals. Your goal areas may look different. For example, you might want to separate your Work & Finances goals, or, you may want to make the Family & Friends goals separate.

Whatever list you choose, I suggest making 3 or 4 specific goals in each of the main categories. Here are suggestions to think about.

1. Spiritual

This is a huge area. We are created in God's image and are not just physical, but spiritual beings. Some people suggest meditating in the mornings to get more centered.

For me, my center is rooted in Christianity. I don't believe that this amazingly complex world was created by mere chance. There is definitely an intelligent designer.

Here is where you can have goals around knowing more about God and making goals like attending a good church, etc. This is also where you can write down your character goals. For example, working on traits like kindness, patience, and persistence, etc.

One of my spiritual goals is to read through the Bible every year. I've succeeded in that goal since 1982. When you make a goal, it's best to actually write out your plan of how to achieve it, like the successful Harvard MBA's mentioned earlier in this chapter.

For example, this year I'm using a study Bible by Pastor David Jeremiah. The Jeremiah Study Bible has 1870 pages. To complete it in a year, you divide 1870 by 365 days and I know that by reading 5 or 6 pages a day it will be finished by the end of the year.

A goal should be specific and measurable. That way it's easier to accomplish and to monitor.

2. Friends and Family

We are social beings and need close relationships. It takes planning and work to keep a marriage strong, to connect with your kids, and to deepen friendships.

If you want a good marriage, you might want to attend some marriage retreats, read marriage books, plan date nights, etc. There are some fantastic books on raising kids that can give you ideas on how to be a great parent.

I liked the book *The Seven Laws of the Learner: How to Teach Almost Anything to Practically Anyone* by Bruce Wilkinson. He has great suggestions for not only teaching others but for blossoming personal relationships.

In the book, he gives an example of successfully parenting teenagers that were emotionally drifting. I've used his techniques with my own guitar students and friends and they work great.

One of the techniques is to look for something to sincerely compliment. Tell them what they did and that you are proud to be their 'Dad', 'friend', 'wife', etc. Give them a future vision to live up to and seal it with a touch or hug, whatever is appropriate.

For example, I had a guitar student that sang badly out of tune. I used to make all the students sing, if they were learning songs, then I could help their singing, too. One day he nailed the pitch perfectly so I told him. "Wow Rudy, look at that! You sang that song beautifully. I'm so proud to be your teacher!"

20

He wanted to eventually be in a rock and roll band so I added… "I bet you could even be the lead singer in your band some day. You're so gifted." Then I touched him on the shoulder.

You can change people's lives by encouraging and supporting them. Bruce credits his international ministry to a vision that one of his teachers gave him in Seminary. It was his favorite teacher and every time he wanted to quit, he looked at a note this man had hand written on one of his papers.

How can you be a better husband, wife, parent, friend, son, daughter, uncle, aunt, grandfather, grandmother, and more? This is where you can write down specific goals of how much time you want to spend with the important people in your life and how you can work on making these relationships richer.

As stated earlier, we are social beings and we need to be in relationships with people to help and be helped by. What are your goals for strengthening the relationships in your life with family and friends? Write them down.

3. Health

It's easy to see we are living in a physical body. It does make a difference what you feed that body, how you treat it, and that you give it enough rest. This is where you can write down your diet and exercise goals.

Did you know that you can reverse diseases like cancer and arthritis primarily with a good diet and exercise? Did you know you can avoid most diseases by what you eat and what you think?

Stress can cause a lot of diseases. One of my friends is convinced that her mother died early of cancer because of a major fallout with a close relative. Her mother just kept feeling badly about it and when she got cancer her resistance was too low to fight it. Worry and stress can develop into depression, panic attacks, anxiety, major heart attacks, cancer, etc.

Just a couple years ago, two men I know had heart attacks. Both were in their 50's and looked in great shape. One of them was actually in front of me at a gym class doing an hour's worth of Tabatas. It was a very hard class and I was shocked to see on Facebook that he was in the hospital after a major heart attack.

It happened at the health club shortly after the class. I had already left. Both men told me that after getting out of the hospital they did a radical shift in their diets. Both started consuming more salads and vegetables.

Eating Tips

Here are a few eating tips that you might want to think about. There are plenty of studies out proving that foods with white flour and refined sugar are not good for you. Corn fructose is another item being added to our foods that is not healthy. One tip is to avoid white flour and refined sugars.

One of my goals is to skip sugary desserts unless it is made by a close friend. Then, I will eat a sliver. When you think of the consequences of eating sugar, it's not difficult to say no. I'd rather have energy and avoid diseases by eating well.

Another tip is to eat foods as close to their original state as possible. Hence, it's better to eat an apple than to eat an apple pie with white flour and refined sugar.

It's staggering how many chemicals are being added to our foods. Did you know that there are over 3000 chemicals that are regularly added to our foods? Our bodies just don't know what to do with these man-made chemicals.

Did you know that 70% of all the antibiotics made in the US are used in farm-raised animals? It's no wonder heart attack and cancer rates are so high in this country!

There are many types of diets, but adding whole fruits and vegetables seem to be a common denominator of the best diets. Eat at least 5 servings of vegetables and 2 servings of fruit each day. They are filled with phytonutrients!

Vitamins were a huge discovery and made popular in the 70's. But it wasn't until the 1990's that phytonutrients were discovered. They are found only in plants and there are more than 100,000 of them!

Making green smoothies or juicing is an excellent way to add more fruits and vegetables to any diet. With a powerful blender like the Vitamix, Blendtec, or even a NutriBullet, you can make it fast and easy.

There is an interesting movie called *Fat, Sick, and Nearly Dead.* It's about an Australian man who traveled across the US filming his juice fast. He was very overweight. Not only did he lose the weight, he also got rid of his rare skin condition/auto immune condition that resulted in nasty rashes. It's an inspiring movie.

He did the juice fast with a Doctor's supervision. If you're really sick, it's smart to get professional help from a knowledgeable Doctor.

At a recent health convention, I met a woman who cured herself of severe MS by changing to a plant-based diet. She lost 70 pounds and normalized her blood. It's been perfect for the last 10 years. She made the changes a lifestyle.

Exercise Tips

Look for ways to add more movement and activities in your day. Here are some easy tips for adding exercise to your life.

The most important tip is getting the right mindset. How about asking yourself what would happen if you didn't exercise? What's that going to do to you in 10, 20, 30 years? Our bodies do the best with good nutrition, exercise and enough sleep. Your mental attitude is also critical for excellent health.

Having an important reason can help you follow through with your goals. It doesn't matter how old you are or what kind of shape you are in today. You're never too old to start exercising.

I used to run in the mornings at UCLA, years ago. There was an older gentleman, Sam, whose law partner had died of a heart attack. Sam's doctor told him that he had to quit smoking or he wouldn't be around much longer, either. Sam was in his 70's and was getting emphysema.

He quit smoking, then decided to take up running. It wore him out to just walk to the track. After several weeks, he was able to run around the track once. Sam didn't give up and he began running 10K races. A 10K is around 6 miles!

Then he wanted to run a half marathon. He asked us if any of us would run with him. I volunteered and stayed with him for the entire 13 miles. We ran very slow, but he made it!

Can you imagine? He went from barely being able to walk to running a half marathon! We have absolutely incredible bodies that can heal themselves and are made to move.

Running may not be your thing, so here are some other types of exercises.

Rebounding

Have you heard of a rebounder? Dr Paul E. Devore, from the American Society of Bariatric Physicians (doctors dealing with weight loss), says rebounding on a quality rebounder burns 11 times more calories than walking, 5 times more than swimming, and 3 times more than jogging or aerobics.

NASA discovered that oxygen consumption while bouncing was up to 68% higher than while running. Just 10 minutes rebounding is equivalent to a 30-minute jogging session.

Rebounding helps your lymphatic system to drain. This is how our body gets rid of toxins and waste. The lymphatic system doesn't have a pump, like our arterial system. It functions only when we are active.

Being inactive can restrict the lymphatic flow and can cause serious problems. Even gentle bouncing is enough to stimulate your lymphatic system and helps it clear out harmful substances in our bodies. It's safe for all ages.

The rebounders are small and some even fold up. Using a rebounder is a quick way to get exercise when you don't have a lot of time. Get a good quality rebounder like this Needak Rebounder.

Needak Rebounder

Tabatas

If time is limited, you might want to try doing Tabatas. Dr. Tabata discovered in a study in 1996 that short high intensity workouts are more beneficial than longer less intense workouts. They are called Tabatas after Dr. Izumi Tabata. A Tabata just takes four minutes. Here is the break down.

- 20 seconds of the highest intensity you can handle (all-out effort)
- 10 seconds of total rest (no movement)
- Repeat the 20-second "hard" intervals and 10-second "recovery" intervals for a total of eight rounds, which equals just four minutes.

Do a search for Tabatas on YouTube for many examples. There are also a number of Tabata apps.

Other programs of bursts of high intensity are P.A.C.E and HIT. I have Dr. Sears book on P.A.C.E. (Progressively Accelerating Cardiopulmonary Exertion) and it can be done by sprinting, using an exercise bike, treadmill, or any type of exercise where you can exert yourself in small bursts of effort.

Like Dr. Tabata, Dr. Sears discovered that short blasts of effort were more beneficial than longer slower workouts. In his book, he documents twins and how the one working less time, but with shorter higher intensity, lost more weight and gained more muscle than the twin exercising much longer on a treadmill, without the bursts of effort.

Strength Training

In addition to the cardio workouts suggestions above, it's highly recommended to do some strength training with weights. There are several schools of thought, but using slower motions with higher weights works well and just going 6 or 7 repetitions to muscle fatigue can be as beneficial as doing 3 sets of 15 reps.

To achieve the super slow speed in weight lifting, aim for 10 seconds to lift the weight and 10 seconds for lowering. You can use the equipment at any gym. Although, you might want to get a trainer because it's very hard to go to muscle fatigue on each machine.

The entire workout lasts 20 minutes and you will be exhausted. I did this once a week with a trainer and loved when the sessions were over. They were very hard!

Stretching

At a health club a number of years ago, I met a woman who told me that stretching literally helped her get out of a wheelchair. Stretching increases your circulation, increases your range of motion, and helps to reduce stress. It can improve your posture and may even help you to avoid muscle injuries.

My friend, Geri Gates, makes an excellent strap called Stretch-It-Out Strap. Unlike cheap nylon or tubing, they are very durable and last for many years. She has a variety of straps. You can find them in the Resource Section at the back of this book.

Isometric and Resistance Exercises

Isometric exercises can be done anywhere. They are done by tensing muscles against other muscles or against a fixes object.

One example is a plank. A plank is when you hold your body rigid from the elbows to the toes. You can also do a knee plank which is a bit easier than a full plank. You bend your knees and support your body from the elbows to the knees.

Here is a photo of my friend Micah holding a full body plank. Lay on the floor and support yourself with your elbows and toes. The object is to hold it as long as you can. You can use a timer to see how long you can hold it. I suggest starting with 1 minute.

Plank

Here are a couple more isometric exercises you can try. For an isometric pull, clasp your hands together then try to pull them apart. Flip your hands, as shown in the photo on the next page, and pull as hard as you can. Hold each for around 10 seconds.

These particular exercises can be done at any age. Even a great-grandmother I know in her late 90's enjoys doing the exercises shown on the next few pages.

Isometric Pull

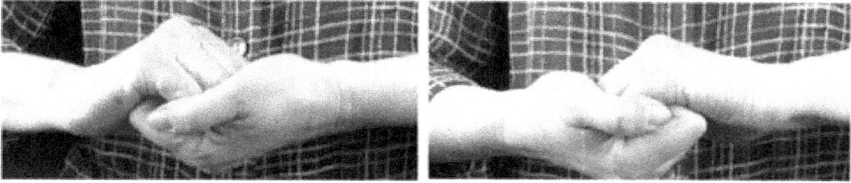

Next, you can try the opposite. Press your palms together and push as hard as you can. Flip them as shown in the picture below and push again, holding for around 10 seconds.

Isometric Push

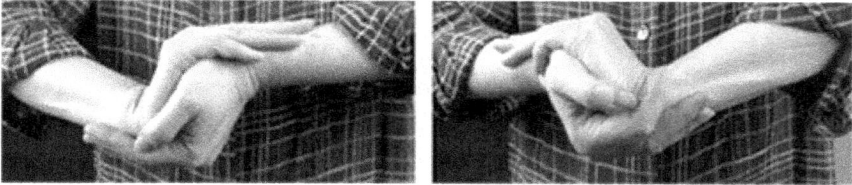

The next one is done by making 2 fists and pushing one fist away as you pull the opposite fist towards you. Then, you can reverse the hands. This will work both sets of muscles. It works your biceps and triceps.

Isometric Push and Pull

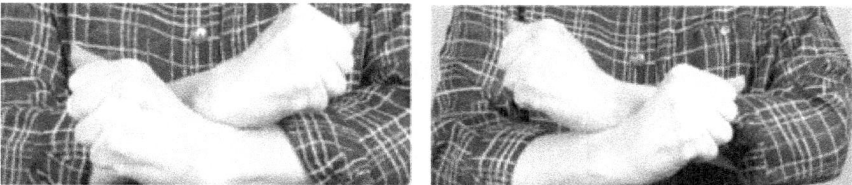

Isometrics are usually a static holds, but years ago I read

about using resistance without weights. For example, you can pretend that you're holding heavy weights. Then, tense your whole body while lifting the imaginary weights. It's important to breathe and not hold your breath. Tighten your whole body. Here is an example of lifting an imaginary weight.

Mental Body Resistance

Start with your arm to your side. Make a fist, tighten your whole body, and pretend you are lifting a heavy weight. You can use resistance both lifting your arm up and returning your arm back down. You can use the arms individually, or both together at the same time.

At a recent health seminar, I met Wendie Pett. She has a very good program called Visibly Fit™. Like the previous examples, with her program your body is your gym and the exercises can be done anywhere.

Her program uses slow-controlled tension/resistance movements. You get a good workout without putting stress on your joints, tendons, or ligaments. Wendie messed up her shoulder in a snowmobile accident and used her exercises to heal it without surgery.

Other Exercise Ideas

Please don't neglect exercising. You'll have more energy and sleep better by adding consistent exercise into your routine. Perhaps you have other exercise goals. My parents loved to square dance every Friday night, golf, and go for walks during the week.

I enjoy hiking and walking as well. Other sports you might want to consider include pilates, swimming, biking, martial arts, surfing, skiing, tennis, using an exercise ball, etc. Find something you enjoy doing and make it a regular part of your day.

Can you walk with a friend or neighbor? Gardening and house cleaning also count towards exercise when you work at it. If you have a job that requires you to sit all day, stand up every 20 minutes and stretch or walk around. We were made to move and sitting or laying down for extended periods is not healthy.

4. Work & Finances

I have always loved my work. Each of us has specific talents and when you can actually match your talent to your work and you love what you do, bravo!

You may want to think about what you enjoy doing and your skill sets. We all come into this world without much knowledge. If you put your heart and actions into it, you can learn essentially any skill, even if you don't have a natural talent for it.

A quick story. I had two young boys studying guitar. Steve was a very slow learner and didn't seem to have much talent. My next door neighbor, on the other hand, picked up songs very fast and he had so much natural talent.

I assumed Rodney would go far, but after a couple months, he quit. Little Steve continued lessons for a number of years. He could play circles around Rodney.

It's not how talented you are, but that you don't quit. It doesn't matter how quickly you learn, just don't quit.

I think of Colonel Harland Sanders who at age 60 had to close his restaurant because of a new highway. At the age of 65 he decided to franchise his chicken recipe. One thousand nine people turned him down before he got his first yes.

He had a passion and a vision and didn't stop with any of the 1009 negative responses. Now KFC, Kentucky Fried Chicken, is one of the largest fast food franchises in the world.

Summer months were always very slow for teaching guitar, so early in my career I was determined to make my career work. I have a Master's degree in Guitar Performance and much of my income was from performing.

During one very slow season, I decided to make 30 phone calls a day to caterers and places that hired performers. For a whole month I only heard the word: "No." But, a few people did request a brochure. The next month, my phone began to ring and all those calls paid off.

Here is where you can also make specific income goals. You can figure out how much you need to make per year, month, week and even day to reach the goal. Then, you'll know what to do each day to reach it.

Are you happy with your work? Your income? Make a plan, then only focus on the solution and not the problem. Make a plan, then work your plan. Write your goals down plus how you plan on achieving them. Focusing on problems will only drain you and make it harder to get moving.

There are some interesting new books out about setting and implementing goals like *The Miracle Morning: The Not-So-Obvious Secret Guaranteed to Transform Your Life (Before 8AM)* or *The 12 Week Year: Get More Done in 12 Weeks than Others Do in 12 Months.* Check out the Resources at the back of this book or online at **GraciousPublishing.com/resources**

We talked about stress in the last chapter. Worry about lack of finances is one of the major causes of stress. This is where making goals and focusing on achieving your goals instead of dwelling on your problems will make a huge difference. I like this quote by Zig:

> *"You can have everything in life you want, if you will just help enough other people get what they want."*
> *Zig Ziglar*

If you work for someone else, how can you add more value to your job? You should get paid more when you add more value.

I've hired a number of people to help in my business and the ones that actually took initiative to do more than I asked were a particular joy to work with.

In the movie 'Steve Jobs', they brought out the fact that Steve, the founder of Apple Computer, always had the end user in mind. He wanted the user to have a better experience and his products to be easy for them to use.

If you are self-employed, what can you do to enrich the lives of your customers? How else can you serve them?

With my guitar teaching business, I used to set aside the first day of the year to just pray and ask what else I could do in my business. One year I came up with seven different complementary businesses based around my skills. I ended up implementing six of them.

5. Service/Community

If you want a happy fulfilled life, find places to serve. Seriously, God gives us gifts and talents to be a blessing to others. I mentioned how relationships are so very important, more important than even how much money you make.

In the Bible, there is a passage that says it is more blessed to give than to receive. There is another one that says when you give you will receive even more than you gave.

There are many ways to give. You can give your time, your stuff, or your money. You can serve in your church or community.

In my 20's, I was taking voice lessons and at the end of one of the lessons, my voice teacher showed me a catalog that had just come in the mail. They owned several acres of property in Topanga Canyon and grew lots of their own food.

The ground was very hard and she pointed to a picture of a Troy-Bilt rototiller. She mentioned how she wished they could afford it. It would have made it much easier to till the ground. I thought of buying one for them, but didn't have that kind of money, either.

My teacher headed the Lute Society of America, so I called some of the other members and around 25 of us pitched in to buy her the rototiller. It took a few months to raise the money and then for it to be delivered. But, at the end I was so excited that I couldn't sleep. I couldn't wait to see the surprise on her face. I served by organizing this gift of love.

Another quick story: I was in a music store once and saw a

gentleman looking at guitar instructional books. He looked a bit baffled, so I came over and gave him my opinion of the best book to start with and why. I also gave him a few tips on playing the guitar to help him get started.

Because I was so knowledgeable and helpful, he ended up taking lessons with me. That was not my goal, but when you help people there is always a blessing. Sometimes the blessing comes from completely different sources.

Keep your ears open for opportunities to be a blessing in the lives of the people around you. Any new moms in the neighborhood? How about bringing them a meal for the family?

Steve Sjogren has written a number of books on acts of kindness. One is called *Changing the World Through Kindness*. Pastor Steve started a church in Cincinnati, Ohio. It just didn't grow until they began going into the neighborhood with acts of kindness.

They started a soup kitchen, then just looked for ways to serve the community. They did things like putting money in expired meters and offering to paint and clean schools. When they focused on serving, the church exploded with growth.

Remember I mentioned earlier about how we are social beings. I would love for you to connect up with a good church, or organization that focuses on helping people. It can add immeasurable riches to your life.

One of the highlights of my week is serving in a number of ministries in my church. In serving, I've gotten to know lots of new people and have forged wonderful friendships in the process.

Look for ways to serve the people around you. It will make your life richer and happier and will change you.

I hope these goal ideas are helpful for you in deciding your Life Goals. These should be your priorities when planning out your days.

Here' a fun quote from Stephen Covey:

"The key is not to prioritize what's on your schedule, but to schedule your priorities." - Stephen Covey

Action Items

- Carve out a few of hours and think about the goals that are most important to you. Write them down, and then make them measurable. You can use my ideas as a sample.
- Look at your list and then look at your life. What areas do you need to grow in? Think about how to implement your goals and start today.

In this chapter, we looked at having life goals. It's good to have well-rounded goals, not just financial goals. Next, you will learn a method for decluttering your mind. I call it a Brain Dump.

Brain Dump

In the last section, we looked at the importance of well-rounded goals. It's difficult to focus without clear goals. It's also difficult to live an organized life when our minds are filled with so many things that need to be done.

In this chapter, you'll learn an easy technique to free up your mind from all of those distracting thoughts. I like to call it a Brain Dump. It's finding a system to get all of those miscellaneous ideas out of your head and to capture them by writing them down.

A perfect solution for worry or for major decisions is to write it down on paper and then think about the solutions. Once you have the solutions in mind and written down, focus on what you are going to do and not the problem. Then, take steps towards implementing the solutions.

I love this quote from Corrie ten Boom. Corrie's family, in Holland, helped smuggle Jews to safety during WWII. Her story is in the book and movie is called *The Hiding Place*. They were captured and sent to a concentration camp. Corrie survived and traveled the world speaking and encouraging everyone who would listen. Here is one of her famous quotes:

"Worry does not empty tomorrow of its sorrow; it empties today of its strength." - Corrie ten Boom

That is so true. Worrying won't help anything and can harm you. It's one of the body's ways to get our attention, but not to live there.

If you have work or business ideas, write them down. Don't lose those great ideas.

Tools

You need a place to capture all those thoughts. The easiest is to use a notebook with paper. I don't suggest single sheets of paper because it's so easy to lose. Have a spiral notebook, or something that can be a bit more permanent.

Another option is to just dump all of your thoughts and ideas into lists in something like Microsoft Word. One of my very productive friends uses this method with much success. Both Mac and PC's have word processing programs that can work well.

In addition, there are applications available specifically for organizing your ideas. I've used and can recommend Things, OmniFocus, or Nozbe. Both Things and OmniFocus are only available for Macs. Nozbe works on all operating systems, but does have a small monthly or yearly charge.

All three have an 'Inbox'. You can put all of your ideas into the InBox. Then, you can move them into 'Scheduled' items, 'Someday' items or into 'Projects'. Things for Mac or Nozbe are a bit easier to learn than OmniFocus. OmniFocus has more features. I'll show you all three.

In Things, there is a folder called 'Today' which is where you can put the tasks you want completed that day. Plus, the tasks with dates attached will automatically appear in 'Today'.

'Someday' is a catchall for ideas that you aren't doing now but want to do in the future. Here is a screenshot of Things from their website:

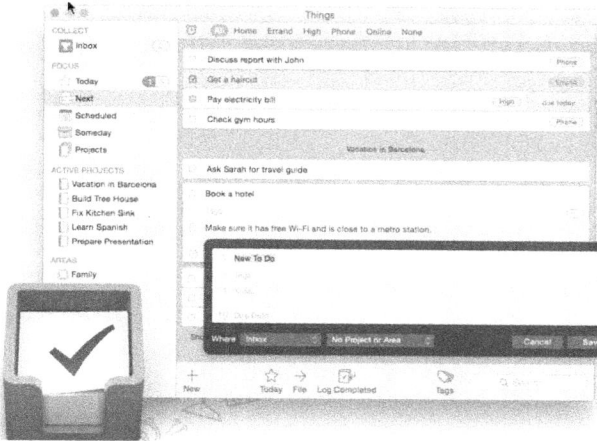

Here is a screenshot of OmniFocus from their website:

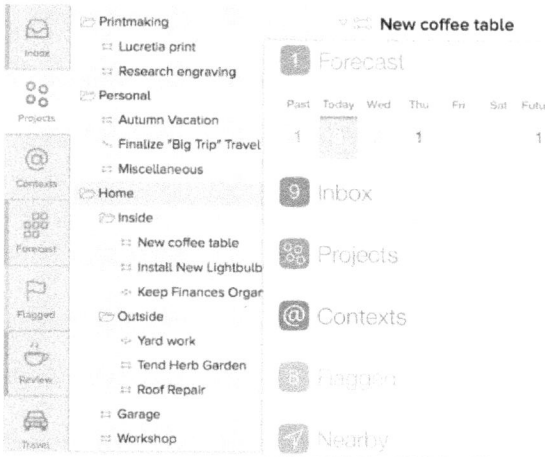

In any good organizer tasks can be repeated. This is perfect for remembering to pay bills, taxes, and to remember birthdays and anniversaries. You can also set up recurring reminders in online calendars. They can be set up to remind you a few days before the events.

OmniFocus has all of the features of Things plus the ability to Review your projects at a set time that you determine. The 'Forecast' view can pull in all of the activities from your online calendar so you can see what's coming up.

Both Things and OmniFocus have apps for iPads and iPhones so you can use them on any Mac Platform. Nozbe also has apps, but for any operating system. Plus, Nozbe works in any web browser.

At the time of writing of this book, Things costs around $50, OmniFocus costs $40 for their standard edition and $80 for the pro edition. Nozbe is free for 1 user with 5 projects. For unlimited projects and 2 members it's around $8 a month. Check the Resources section at the back of the book for a 10% discount code for Nozbe.

Nozbe integrates at the API level to several other productivity tools. This includes Evernote, DropBox, Google Drive, Box, and Google Calendar. When adding a comment on any task, you have the option to include any file from these platforms. The time saved is huge and since I do use 3 of the 5 platforms, I've switched over to Nozbe. Here is a screenshot from their website.

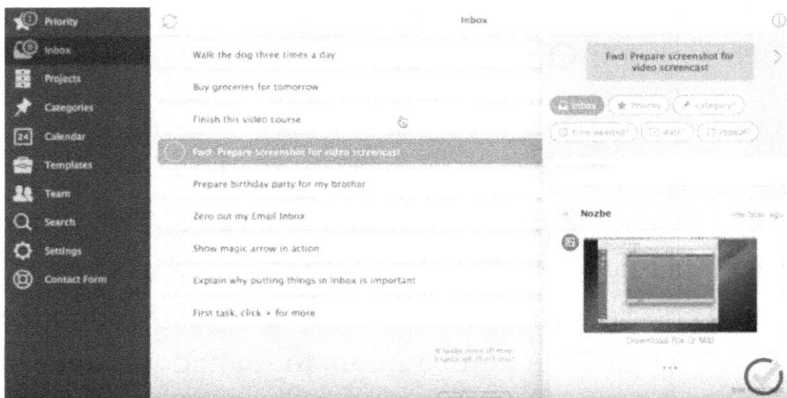

I have also used Trello. Trello is good tool for working on specific projects. It uses boards, where you can add item To-Dos. You can add as many boards to a project as you want. Each board can hold an unlimited amount of To-Dos.

The premise is to add all the To-Dos in the far left column. As they are being worked on or completed, just manually drag them to the right. As you can see in this screenshot from their website, you can also add pictures to the boards.

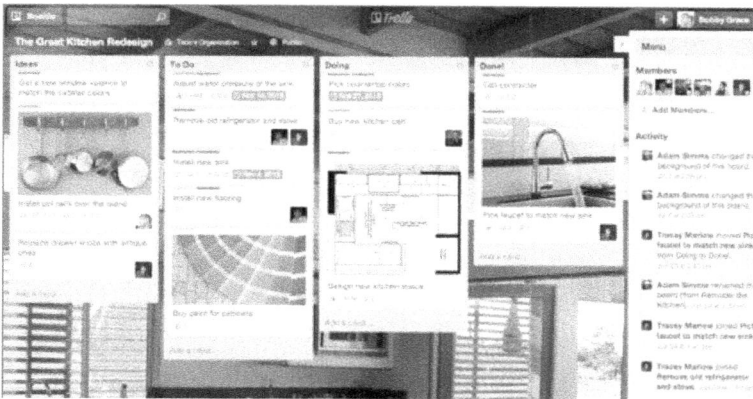

What's special about Trello, besides being free, is that you can add people to a board and track what is being done. It is web-based and will work on any platform with Internet access.

This is great for single projects and working with teams, but I don't think it's the best place for a major Brain Dump.

Trello uses a process called kanban. A kanban means 'signboard' in Japanese and was first invented by Mr. Onho for Toyota, in the 1940's.

It's an effective way to keep track of production and inventory. A kanban is more an execution tool than a planning tool. There are both physical kanban boards and software applications built just for implementing the kanban process.

Another excellent tool to use is Evernote. It is not a

management program like the Nozbe. It's a place to capture and store articles and ideas.

Evernote syncs over any device including Windows, Macs, smartphones and tablets of all types. It is great for storing photos, audios, web clippings, notes, and more.

I use Evernote for storing information that I use often or for capturing ideas that I want available on more than one device. You can make the notes private or public.

Other web-based To-Do platforms that are good options are Producteev, Wrike, and Asana. You can access these with a Mac, PC, or anything that has an Internet connection.

Asana is free for up to 15 users and Wrike also has a free option for 5 users. Wrike and Asana are good for working with teams.

Brain Dumps are not just a one time event. When you have some systems in place, you can continue to update them with whatever comes up or is on your mind. For example, when emails come in that I need to take action on, they are forwarded to a special email address that shows up in my Nozbe Inbox.

If it's an email that has information I want to keep for the future and doesn't require any actions, I forward it to my Evernote account.

If I get a phone call or remember something that needs attention, with a couple clicks of the mouse, a box shows up and I can send the ideas straight into Nozbe. Nothing falls through the cracks.

I hope you are beginning to see how useful and easy it is to do Brain Dumps. They can help you to focus without worrying about forgetting important ideas or events. Then, with a system in place, you can continue to use it whenever anything pops into your head. This frees your mind to work on one thing at a time.

Worry and stress are areas to work on eliminating. According to webmd.com, 75 to 90% of all doctor visits are caused by stress-related ailments and complaints. An excellent cure to worry is focusing on the solutions and not the problems.

Focus On Solutions, Not Problems

Remember to focus on the solution, not the problem. Focusing only on the problem can make you sick. There are a couple Bible verses that I have found extremely beneficial at times when I have felt stressed. The first is from the book of Philippians.

> *Do not be anxious about anything, but in every situation, by prayer and petition, with thanksgiving, present your requests to God. And the peace of God, which transcends all understanding, will guard your hearts and your minds in Christ Jesus. Philippians 4:6,7*

> *Cast all your anxiety on him because he cares for you. 1 Peter 5:7*

All through the Old and New Testament we are called sheep. We aren't called donkeys or horses. We are called sheep. Sheep aren't made to carry burdens.

When you do your Brain Dump, if you find things on your mind that are particularly hurtful or stressful, I recommend taking them in prayer to the One who created you in the first place. Sometimes it's very appropriate to go through a time of grieving. But, often our thoughts can be too negative when it's not necessary.

I have heard that it takes 10 positive thoughts to undo one negative thought. I'm not sure if this is true, but I have seen that dwelling on negative thoughts can get you depressed and if you stay there, it's not helpful.

I went to a seminar a number of years ago and learned a little trick that can be helpful in getting out of a negative cycle. When people are depressed, they tend to look down and slump over.

Here are a couple easy to follow steps that can help most anyone get out of a negative frame of mind. It's so easy to do and takes just a few minutes. Here are the steps to use:

- Sit down, look down, and think of the problem that's on your mind.
- Make it bigger and closer.
- Then, jump up, look up, and think of an event that made you very happy. It could something from a recent activity or even in the past. Maybe an award you received or an amazing sunrise. It helps to also verbally express your joy with a word like "YES!"
- With good posture, walk around and make the happy event bigger, brighter, and closer.
- Repeat these steps. Sit down and focus on the problem, then jump up and walk around focusing on something that has made you very happy. Make it bigger and brighter in your mind.
- Try to repeat it one or two more times. What you'll find is that it will become impossible to even get depressed.

I love to use this little exercise with friends that get stuck in an unhealthy negative attitude. Oh, it's very good to look at the negatives in situations, but don't camp out there.

Another neat trick to use when negative thoughts just won't leave you is to make them smaller and further away in your mind. Make them very tiny and very far away.

It's best to simply replace them with a positive thought. This helps to diminish the negative effects that negative thoughts can have on your well being.

Look at your Brain Dump list and categorize the items into things you need to take care of now, things for the future, things that others can do, and items to discard.

When planning your day, don't forget your Life Goals. Often the urgent items gets our attention, but we need to carve out time for all areas of our lives. For example, it would be easy to not exercise or take care of your health.

You can use a calendar to mark off chunks of time for things you want to accomplish. Google Calendars work well and can be synced over all devices. Windows and Mac operating systems both ship with useful calendars.

Don't want to use a computer? Day Timers is what I used to use, but I found Planner Pads to be even better. You can see a week at a time and the To-Dos can be better organized. I ended up making 2 sheets for each week that used the ideas from Planner Pads with a twist. Instead of three rows, two rows worked better for me.

An example is shown here:

Monday	Tuesday	Wednesday	Thursday
9.	9:	9:	9:
10.	10:	10:	10:
11:	11:	11:	11:
12:	12:	12:	12:
1:	1:	1:	1:
1:30.	1:30:	1:30:	1:30:
2:	2:	2:	2:
2:30	2:30	2:30	2:30
3:	3:	3:	3:
3:30	3:30	3:30	3:30
4:	4.	4.	4.
4:30	4:30	4:30	4:30
5:	5:	5:	5:
5:30	5:30	5:30	5:30
6:	6	6	6
6:30:	6:30:	6:30.	6:30:
7:	7:	7:	7:

At the beginning of the week, I put the appointments for each day and saw where there were chunks of time for working. Then, either the night before or in the morning, I planned out the To-Dos of the next day. Check the Resource Section at the back for downloading these sheets free.

Now, I capture everything in Nozbe and love that it's on the computer. If your thoughts were only written on paper, when you turn a page, they can get lost.

Other Internet tools that you might find helpful are:

Dropbox - A great place to store files. You can give certain people permission to access the files. This is perfect if you have a team of workers. It's a safe place where you can send and receive large files.

ManageWP - A single place to manage all of your Wordpress blogs. When you log in, you can update all the blogs with one click. This is a HUGE time saver and can help to keep your websites from being hacked.

46

Lastpass or 1Password are both good tools to remember the passwords of all the websites you use. I do not think it's a good idea to store passwords of financial website, like your bank. Keep those memorized.

Free Your Mind

Brain Dumping is not a one time action. Our brains are constantly coming up with things to remember, new ideas, etc. Having a system to capture all your ideas will free your mind.

Even at night, I suggest having a little recorder, paper, or an electronic device, like a smartphone, with you to quickly capture your thoughts.

Keep something with you all the time, to capture your ideas. As a musician, I've often thought of lyrics or a melody for a song. When inspired, I have to immediately record it, or it's lost. I've written a number of songs because they were captured in the early stages.

If you are in the middle of a project and remember something you need to do, simply write it down and go back to the project at hand.

If you do not write it down, it may continue to distract you or you might be frustrated later when you can't remember what it was. Again, I just use a few keystrokes to instantly put any thoughts or ideas into Nozbe.

Your mind can be like an empty Inbox with all the To-Do items neatly stored in memory folders and off the desktop of the immediate project. Doesn't that sound freeing? It is!

Mindset

One of the skills that organized people cultivate is making decisions. In the book *Getting Things Done* by Robert Allen, he emphasizes capturing everything that needs to get done into a system and discipling yourself to make front-end decisions.

He suggests that if you can do something in 2 minutes or less, do it now. This applies to both paper clutter and emails. He says to have everything you need at hand. For example, all the items you'll need on a desk like pens, paper clips, etc.

My friend, Nancy, shared one of her biggest organizational tips. Nancy works full time and has 6 kids. When she got her new job, she told us that she prayed and prayed that God would help her to be extremely organized at work.

She said her biggest tip was to just do anything that takes a few minutes without adding them to your To-Do list first. The goal is to keep that list very short and just immediately act on items that can be done quickly.

Nancy credits God for the tremendous favor she's experiencing and how very organized she is at work. Her boss even told her that she would make a very good supervisor and to please apply for that position!

If you need to make a decision with various options. You can take out a sheet of paper, divide it into sections, and write down the pros and cons of each option. Then, make a decision. Here's a fun and appropriate quote about decisions.

"Clutter is nothing more than postponed decisions."
Barbara Hemphill

Some people get stuck in the analyzing phase and never move into acting on the decisions. You can get stuck for a very long time. It's better to make a decision then change it down the road.

When you really can't decide, go with your gut feelings. Steve Jobs often talked about trusting his intuition.

"Have the courage to follow your heart and intuition. They somehow already know what you truly want to become. Everything else is secondary."
Steve Jobs

As a Christian, I like to write down the options and then pray over them. When I was first going to make my guitar instructional videos I was told by a Christian Store Manager that they wouldn't sell and no one was asking for guitar instructional videos. He advised me not to make them and that it would be a waste of money. But, if I made them he would take a few.

I prayed for an extended period and knew I was supposed to make them. I even wrote down 70 ideas of what to put in them and how to market them.

Fast forward, the same gentleman who told me not to make them told me that they were selling in all of their stores and that I should turn them into DVD's and include a Spanish track. He said that they would probably do well nationwide.

For big decisions, it's a good idea to get outside input, then follow your gut feelings. Make decisions and take actions now.

Besides making decisions, guard your thoughts. I saw an interesting video from a brain specialist about how our thoughts affect our brains. It's possible to rewire your brain. Every thought that we think impacts the 75 to 100 trillion cells in our body. Your brain can be changed by your thinking. It's called Neuroplasticity.

It was thought that our brain couldn't create new neurons and that when a cell died no new cell could replace it. Now we know that our brains can indeed create new neurons and how we think does impact our brain. Even the elderly can grow new neurons. It is never too late to learn something new!

Your brain is subservient to your mind. According to a talk by Dr. Caroline Leaf, 75% to 98% of current emotional, mental, and physical illnesses today are affected by our thought life, including cancers and other diseases.

That sounds about right because those are the same figures for stress-related disease. Stress and negative thoughts tend to go together like a hand in a glove.

The more you stay in a negative zone, the more vulnerable you become to illnesses. Toxic thoughts lead to a damaged brain. Be aware of your thoughts and how you are thinking.

What you do with your thinking can change the nature of your brain. I have often equated this to food. There is nothing you eat that does not count.

The same reaction of your body to a cut happens when you have toxic thoughts. When you change your mind, your brain can regrow.

Carolyn worked with kids with very bad learning disabilities in South Africa. She has seen them get degrees and become top spokespeople in their industries. Even with major brain damage, the brain cells can be rebuilt.

You can't control the events in your life, but you can control your reaction to them. Guard your thoughts. We can only think about one thing at a time. Replace negative thoughts with ones that are uplifting and inspiring. Shift how you view circumstances. This is a great quote from Mr. Lincoln

> *"We can complain because rose bushes have thorns, or rejoice because thorn bushes have roses."*
> *Abraham Lincoln*

Being organized starts with your mindset. What do you do if there are hurtful thoughts? In the next section, we'll look at ways to handle hurt and unforgiveness.

Freedom in Forgiveness

Corrie ten Boom, who was quoted earlier in this book, made an astute observation about forgiveness. Her family helped many Jews escape the Nazi Holocaust during World War II. After helping so many escape into freedom, they were captured and send to one of the worst concentration camps.

After the war, Corrie opened centers to help the surviving Jews heal and recover from the cruelties in the concentration camps. She observed that the ones who refused to forgive just never got better.

If you have been wronged or are holding unforgiveness towards anyone, it can negatively impact you both physically and mentally. What we think about can affect our physical well being. Plus, by holding onto unforgiveness, you are giving them too much mental space.

Jesus said not only to forgive but in the book of Matthew He said to love your enemies:

"You have heard that it was said, 'Love your neighbor and hate your enemy.' But I tell you, love your enemies and pray for those who persecute you, that you may be children of your Father in heaven. He causes his sun to rise on the evil and the good, and sends rain on the righteous and the unrighteous." Matthew 5:43-45

In the camp, Corrie's sister and Father both died. After the war, Corrie traveled to many countries to share about God's faithfulness to them even, inside the concentration camps.

One day she was in Germany and to her surprise, she recognized a man standing in the back. It was one of the guard that had been so cruel to her sister Betsie. I'll let Corrie tell you in her own words what went through her mind.

"It was at a church service in Munich that I saw him, a former S.S. man who had stood guard at the shower room door in the processing center at Ravensbruck. He was the first of our actual jailers that I had seen since that time. And suddenly it was all there – the roomful of mocking men, the heaps of clothing, Betsie's pain-blanched face.

He came up to me as the church was emptying, beaming and bowing. "How grateful I am for your message, Fraulein." He said. "To think that, as you say, He has washed my sins away!" His hand was thrust out to shake mine. And I, who had preached so often to the people in Bloemendaal the need to forgive, kept my hand at my side.

Even as the angry, vengeful thoughts boiled through me, I saw the sin of them. Jesus Christ had died for this man; was I going to ask for more? Lord Jesus, I prayed, forgive me and help me to forgive him. I tried to smile, I struggled to raise my hand. I could not. I felt nothing, not the slightest spark of warmth or charity. And so again I breathed a silent prayer. Jesus, I prayed, I cannot forgive him. Give me Your forgiveness.

As I took his hand the most incredible thing happened. From my shoulder along my arm and through my hand a current seemed to pass from me to him, while into my heart sprang a love for this stranger that almost overwhelmed me. And so I discovered that it is not on our forgiveness any more than on our goodness that the world's healing hinges, but on His. When He tells us to love our enemies, He gives, along with the command, the love itself."
Corrie ten Boom

There are many commands in the Bible that seem impossible. Fortunately, it was written by the One that says nothing is impossible with Him.

I hope you're beginning to see how some of these principles just make sense. Holding onto unforgiveness is not living in a place that will serve you. Being able to forgive and let go of painful pasts is a healthier place to live.

Living in forgiveness is of such huge importance, I wanted to at least touch on the topic for any that may have struggles in this area.

Action Items

- Sit down with your preferred capturing method and write down everything that's on your mind. Write down big things and small things. Need to contact someone? Write it down. Need to fix something? Write it down. Write down everything.
- When you finish, look over the list and make decisions. Is there something there you can do in a couple minutes? Do it now. Are there items that other people should do? Delegate them. Are there some things that really aren't necessary or important? Cross them off or put them on a Someday List.
- Are there things that are weighing you down? Unforgiveness? Deal with them by using some of the ideas in this chapter.
- Use a system to plan out what to do each day. If you would like to use my 2 sheet system, it's available free at: GraciousPublishing.com/resources/

In this section, we looked at freeing up your mind by capturing your thoughts and filtering your To-Dos and projects based on your most important goals. It's good to have your mind free from all clutter.

Being organized starts with your mindset and thinking. Once you are aware of your thoughts, you'll need a physical system to stay organized. Next, we'll look at a system to keep your physical stuff organized.

Organize Your Surroundings

Up to this point, we've been focusing on your inner life. Looking at your goals and thoughts. Now, we'll shift to discussing systems to get and keep your surrounding organized.

Paper System

First, you should set up a system to find papers easily. I suggest getting the following items:

- A file cabinet (This can even be a file cabinet box if you're on a budget)
- A labeler
- Hanging folders
- A program like FileMaker, Paper Tiger or even a spread-sheet like Excel or Google Sheets

You should set up a couple different file systems. For receipts have 12 folders labeled January through December. Then, as you purchase items, toss the receipt in the folder of the month they were purchased. I use QuickBooks now, but used to take out the receipts at the end of the year to see which were tax related.

For larger purchases or purchases with a warranty, I clip the receipt to the manual and put it in the main folder system. Then, if I need to get it fixed, I can quickly find the original receipt for proof of purchase. Keep your receipts for items like camera's, computers, refrigerators, tools, etc.

I don't put those with the rest of the monthly receipts because it would be too time consuming to sort through all the receipts to find them. When the receipts are clipped to the inside cover of the manual, it's not only easier to find, it's less likely to get lost or tossed. You may want to make a copy of the receipt to add to the monthly folders if it is a tax deductible item.

If there are several small papers with the purchase, I put everything in a ziploc bag to keep it all together.

Next, set up the main folder system for all the other papers. You can label folders for 'Health', 'Manuals', 'Auto', and basic categories or you can simply number the labels - 1, 2, 3, 4, etc.

I use the numbering system and also have a few folders labeled. I like to keep my coupons all in one folder and separate folders for 'Banking', 'Health', 'Investments', and 'Auto'.

Use a program like FileMaker to capture what the paper is about, and then what folder number it's in. This is what I did with all the songs I taught. Then, you will never have a folder that is too full and you will know exactly where the next sheet will be filed.

Don't have FileMaker? You could use a service like Paper Tiger. It's specifically made for organizing file cabinet papers. They use the same concept that I have used for years for filing with FileMaker.

In FileMaker, I suggest having 3 or 4 categories. List the item name, a brief description, and where it's stored. You can then easily sort them by name and see where it's located. Here's a screen shot of how I've set up FileMaker for my main capturing system.

Name	Sort Button	Location		Keywords
Apple care protection plan		Garage File #1, D #1	Ref 5	Apple Care protection for
Auto files		Garage File #1, D #1	Ref 1	21st Century, Auto files, Automobile
banner hooks				banner hooks - It's in the garage in
Baroque Guitar Music song list		Garage File #1, D #1	Ref 16	Baroque Guitar Label
Blendtec blender booklet		Garage File #1, D #2	Ref 30	bought July 6 09, Serial #TTBB
Bottom Line Enterprises, Victoria		Garage File #1, D #2	Ref 34	Bottom Line Enterprises, Victoria
Bowker's		Garage File #2, D #2	Ref 30	Bowker's video directory
Brian Moore Guitars, Inc.		Garage File #1, D #2	Ref 26	Brian Moore Guitars, Inc. invoice

I use the Name of the item, the Location, folder number, and lots of Keywords. The Keyword fields open up when you click into the field. You can add any words that may make it easier for you to remember and find later.

Since I have more than one file cabinet and in more than one place, I like to specify in the Location Column where the cabinet is located. There are two in the garage, so I labeled them Garage File #1 and #2. The 'D' stands for the drawer. Both cabinets have 4 drawers. The 'Ref' is the folder number. I may have a dozen or more different papers in each folder.

The 'banner hooks', in the screenshot above, don't go in a file cabinet, but I've specified where they are in the garage because they were an item I needed to quickly locate for Trade Shows. The field expands to say where in the garage they are located. Can you see how a system like this can help you get and stay organized?

For the songs I taught, I used 2 categories. Since I already knew which file cabinet they are in, I just added the name and folder number. Then, I could look up the name of the song I wanted to teach, and quickly find it in the numbered folder it was stored in.

In addition, I made an alphabetical printout of all of the songs and put it in the front folder so I didn't have to look it up on the computer. None of the folders were too full and the system could be easily expanded by adding more numbered folders.

For numbering the folders, a good labeler comes in handy. It's easier to read the labels when neatly typed. Plus, the labels are sticky and can be applied anywhere.

Does it take time to set up? Yes. But, it will make your life simpler in the long run and is worth doing. I suggest setting up the guts of the system and if you don't have a large block of time to implement it, just start now and do a little each day. Plus, use your new system for anything new that needs to be organized.

You may want to look through your file cabinet drawers at least once a year to purge items you no longer need.

Physical Mail

For postal mail, have these 3 or 4 items ready when sorting the mail.

- Trash or Recycling Container
- Shredder
- Inbox for Taking Actions
- Basket for Filing

When you pick up your mail, have a recycling bin or trash basket handy. You can usually tell by the outside of the letter or mailer if you want to open it. Most should be tossed. We recycle paper in our city, so I have a blue recycling container to dump letters and plastic in. It's next to my trash basket.

For getting rid of papers with sensitive data, use a shredder. Unfortunately, we live in an era where ID Theft is not uncommon. Definitely shred anything with your social security number on it. It's not a bad idea to also shred items with your credit card number.

You can toss anything that can be found easily on the Internet. This includes all the catalogs you get. You can also opt-out of receiving catalogs by contacting the companies.

If you have papers that need to be worked on soon, they can be acted on immediately or go in a letter tray Inbox for things that take longer than 2 minutes. If they are dated actions like bills to pay, add reminders to your calendar or organizational software when to pay them.

For papers you want to keep, simply put them into your paper system set up from the suggestions above.

I don't personally do this, but have heard some people are moving towards being paper-free. With a scanner and Evernote, you can keep everything in the Cloud. All of your papers can be accessible through the Internet.

Try making it a game to see how fast you can sort your mail.

Your Desk

Have a messy desktop? Try these easy steps:

- Take everything off your desk.
- Clean your desktop with a soft cloth and furniture polish

or water.

- Look at each item and only bring back the items you use every day, like your computer.
- Buy desktop organizers for neatly storing pens and note pads, etc.
- Can some of the items be put in a drawer?
- Sort through any papers, as we've already covered. Make decisions on each paper and do one of the following.
  1. Toss it
  2. Do it now
  3. Delegate it to someone else
  4. Put it in the Inbox
  5. File it

Just like sorting the mail, if it's easy to find the information again, toss it. When you finish each day, clear your desk. Then you won't feel so overwhelmed the next day. When working at your desk, work on only one item at a time.

Use an Inbox for things that need to be worked on that take more than 2 minutes. Then, add the task to your To-Do organizer so it gets done.

If there is a bill or something that needs to be done by a specific date, put a note in your To-Do organizer or calendar on a specific date so it's not forgotten, and then file it.

Or, even better, most bills can be set up to be paid automatically. Then, there is no need to schedule it.

Keep your workspace clear of everything except the current project. You'll be more focused without clutter distracting you. My good friend Marion from HealedHealthyandWhole.com has this tip:

"As a writer, when I sit down to begin a project, the first thing I do is clean up my physical space. Decluttering my environment is how I prepare. Then, when I finally sit down at my desk and everything around me is in order, my spirit is calm, my mind is clear and I'm able to focus completely on my writing."
Marion M. Pyle

Your Drawers

Organize your desk and kitchen drawers. The easiest way to organize your drawers is to take everything out and get containers to hold your items you want to keep. There are organizers specially made for all types of drawers: office, kitchen, bathroom, garage, etc. Here are a few simple steps to follow for organizing your drawers.

- Empty the drawer.
- Organize the items.
    1. Toss items that are expired or broken.
    2. Determine if the rest still belong in that drawer.
    3. Sort items by categories like pens and pencils.
- Clean the drawer with a damp cloth.
- Measure the empty drawer.
- Check for containers online, or at a store. Be sure to take the measurements and measuring tape with you.
- Put the items into the drawers, neatly organized inside their new containers.

It's easier to find items in an organized drawer and it looks better too! There is even a store dedicated to supplying containers of all types and sizes. It's called The Container Store and sells both in physical locations and online.

Here is a sample office drawer with dividers. You may recognize one as being the same that is commonly used for silverware in your kitchen.

I also use Ziploc bags for organizing some items that can fit in drawers. Jewelry boxes, for example, have never worked for me. My necklaces have always gotten tangled in them.

Today I use Ziploc bags for each necklace, or piece of jewelry. Then, put the individual bags into larger bags of like types.

For example, the silver necklaces are all in one large Ziploc bag. Each silver necklace is in its own smaller Ziploc bag. I've got one drawer for all of my jewelry. Nothing gets tangled and it's easy to find.

I use this same technique for all of my extra cables and cords. For example, all the USB cables are in one large Ziploc bag, all the Fire-wire cables are together, etc. I label all of the bags so it's easy to find.

Here's a photo of the extra USB cables. It's easy to label with a labeler.

All my extra cables and cords are in one drawer. They used to be tangled all together, but now each has it's own Ziploc bag and I no longer have to sort through a pile of cords to find the specific ones I need.

Besides extra cable and cords. The electrical cords and cables you are using can be a mess under your desk. Here are some ideas of how to eliminate that problem.

All Those Tangled Cords?

It's good to have all of your extra cords organized, but what about the ones you're using? That's when a labeler can come to the rescue! Label all those cords under your computer desk, and anywhere it may be hard to know what device the cord belongs to.

With the labels, it's easy to see what cord belongs to the

printer, the fax, the monitor, etc. Then, if you have to call Tech Support and they tell you to unplug a specific device, it sure is easy to find which plug to pull when they are all labeled! You can also label the various cables.

Here is a photo to give you an idea. You can easily read the labels and know what they each one belongs to. I use labels for all the outlets in my office.

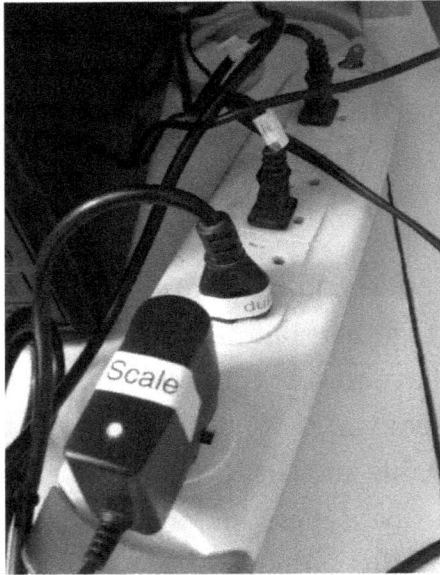

To clean up the mess of cords under your desk, you can bunch loose cords in something like a cable corral, or Velcro. Then, you can get them off the floor or out of sight, and organized.

These are some ideas for getting rid of clutter in your office space. Remember to always toss or giveaway items you don't use. Just organize the stuff that is still useful for you and find a permanent home for each item.

Other Storage Places

Since I had gotten so frustrated with misplacing items, I also added other storage places into FileMaker, not just the file cabinets, for example the banner hooks. This included book cabinets, desk drawers, and more. I added items that could easily be misplaced and that I knew I'd need to find later.

What could have taken hours, now just takes just minutes to find. For example, I recently needed to find my passport. Instead of trying to remember where it was, and looking at a dozen different places, I opened up FileMaker and the 'My Stuff' database, quickly searched for 'passport', and saw exactly where it was located.

All your stuff needs a consistent home. Here's an idea for your keys. Put them in a special place the moment you walk in the door. You can use a key rack or basket. It's also a very good idea to have a spare set of house and car keys in a drawer or other hidden place.

Forget who you lent items to? You can take a photo with your smartphone of the person holding the item they are borrowing. Then, you will have a record of who borrowed your book, your sweater, your music, etc.

Ever misplace your glasses or sunglasses? It's easy to mindlessly put glasses down and then forget where you put them. Decide in advance on where you want to store them. How about putting your sunglasses close to your keys? If you use a basket by the front door, that would be a good place for both. Also, keep an extra set of sunglasses in your car.

For regular or reading glasses, have one or two spots and don't put them anywhere else. Think of where you use them the most. That's the best place to store any item.

If for reading, how about on a tray near your reading chair? If you wear glasses all day, how about on a stand by your bed? Decide in advance to only put your glasses down in specific places.

There are also ways to remember where you have items by using visualization techniques. As you put an item down, see it blowing up or catching on fire in your mind. The more vivid the picture, the more likely you will remember it.

Need to take items the next day to work? Put them on the floor right in front of the door. Write down in your To-Do list to remember to bring items to an event, to work, etc. An even better solution is to put them in the trunk of your car.

Your Closet

For your closet, toss or give away items that no longer fit or that you no longer wear. I like using thin velvet hangers which keep the clothes from slipping and allow you to hang more items.

Then, organize your clothes by type and color. Put all the short sleeve shirts together, all the pants together, etc. When it's organized, you can find things faster.

One method I've heard to help you thin down your closet is to hang all of your garments with the hanger facing out. As you wear items, return them to your closet with the hangers facing in.

Then, after one year, weed out all the of clothes with the hangers facing out. If you haven't worn something in a year, odds are it's not going to be worn next year either.

What I like to do is to go through my closest about once a year and ask four questions about each item.

- Does it fit?
- Is it comfortable?
- Is this something I would wear again?
- Do I love it?

There are a couple sweater vests I hadn't worn for a few years that I just started wearing again this year. They passed all four criteria and I'm glad they were still in my closet.

There are a couple popular books out by Marie Kondo on tidying up. She recommends literally taking everything out of a closet, etc, and only saving the items that spark joy in you. She has an excellent way of folding clothes that makes it easy to see each item. Check out her videos on YouTube.

Here are the specific actions you can take from this chapter for organizing your surroundings.

Action Items

- Make decisions quicker.
- If something takes less than 2 minutes, do it now.
- Set up a system for receipts. (12 Folders, one for each month.)
- Set up a main filing system in FileMaker, Paper Tiger, or a Spreadsheet.
- Clear your desk of all clutter.
- Organize all of your paperwork into your system.
- Sort and toss mail when you first pick it up.
- Organize the messiest, most visible places first.
- Then, tackle your drawers, closet, etc.
- Find containers to help you organize drawers, etc.
- Label cords.
- Make it a lifestyle.

When organizing projects look overwhelming, you can set a timer for just 10 minutes. It's surprising how much can get done and it's not hard to find 10 minutes. Once you get started, it's OK to extend the time longer.

Be patient with yourself. As they say, Rome wasn't built in a day. Start working on these ideas and don't quit. You'll begin to see the difference and feel the difference too. Having an organized environment will help you experience clearer thinking.

In the next chapter, we'll take a look at some routines that can help you to be more productive along with other specific tips that can help.

Organize Your Routines

We've looked at getting clutter out of your mind and physical space. Here are some tips on setting up routines that can support some of your goals.

Evening Routines

Here are some suggestions for evening routines. Look back on your day and see if there are things you can do to make it better. What are you happy about in your day? What would you like to change?

Many people find great benefit in using a journal to examine their lives and record their thoughts. You can simply use a physical journal, or use one of the online apps. This is not a Brain Dump. This is time to reflect on who you are as a person. In what areas would you like to improve? Did you exercise? How was your diet? Did you encourage others?

"An unexamined life is not worth living" - Socrates.

How were your thoughts? Were you proactive and working towards your goals? Were you worried and stuck in a mental rut? I love this quote by Martin Luther,

"Pray, and let God worry." - Martin Luther

Once you've examined your day, write down how you can improve tomorrow. What can you change to make it better. Is there anything you would like to add to your tasks as a reminder?

When you finish reflecting on the day, it's a good idea to start preparing for tomorrow.

Make a list of items you want to accomplish tomorrow and prioritize the list. This will help you have a more productive day. I like to review the list again in the morning to fine tune it, but it helps to work on it the evening before.

Next, put out what you are going to wear the next day. Then, you don't have to take time trying to decide what to wear in the morning. If something needs to be ironed, do it the night before.

Get a good night's sleep. If there are projects or thoughts running through your mind, get them out and captured into whatever tool you've chosen as discussed in a previous chapter. This is a good time for a Brain Dump.

To sleep better, try to exercise during the day. You can take a tea like 'Sleepytime', 'Chamomile', 'Lemon Balm Tea', or drink a cup of 'Tart Cherry Juice'. All of these can help you to relax.

Studies have found that blue light-waves suppress melatonin levels. Melatonin is a hormone that our body produces which helps us sleep. Blue light-waves are emitted in high concentration from electronic devices, like computers, and energy efficient light bulbs.

A simple method to help you sleep better is to wear blue-light-wave blocking glasses, at the end of the evening, when using devices like computers. Although, I personally wear these whenever on the computer.

If you wear glasses, there are options that can fit over your frames. Regular ultraviolet-light blocking glasses will not help. They need to block blue-light. Here are some fit over glasses that block the blue-light.

There is even an option to have your prescription glasses include blue wave blocking. This is ideal for glasses specifically made for working at the computer.

Stretching is another good practice to add to your evening routine. I usually go through an evening stretching routine that just takes a few minutes.

At the end of the evening, it's helpful to visualize waking up the next day refreshed and full of energy. Our minds are amazing and what we think does have an effect on how we feel.

If you have trouble falling asleep, just get up and work and read until you feel sleepy. I took a Dale Carnegie class many years ago and read the book *How to Stop Worrying and Start Living*. In the book Dale Carnegie gave example after example of outstanding people who had trouble sleeping. They lived long and fruitful lives.

Thomas Edison slept 4 or 5 hours a night and Albert Schweitzer slept even less. He was a medical doctor during the day and then practiced playing the organ at night. He was a concert organist and also a Christian missionary to Africa. He was awarded the Nobel Prize for Peace in 1952 and lived to the ripe age of 90.

A short quote from the book:

"Remember, no one was ever killed by lack of sleep. Worrying about insomnia usually causes far more damage than sleeplessness."

Ending the evening with self-examination, as already mentioned, is an excellent practice. Ben Franklin had evening rituals. He looked to improve himself every day. Here is the question he asked himself every evening:

"What good have I done today?" - Ben Franklin

Some people need more sleep. Pay attention to how much sleep you need to be fully rested. Then, decide what time to go to bed and start your evening ritual at least an hour before you want to be asleep. If you have an occasional night where you don't get much sleep, don't worry about it.

Typical Evening Routine

- Brain Dump. Are there more ideas or thoughts that need

to be captured?

- Journaling. Review the Day on paper or in an app. Ask what was great about today? What did I learn? What can I improve?
- Prioritize main tasks for the next day.
- Lay out what clothes to wear for the morning.
- Stretch.
- Visualize waking up rested and ready for the next day.
- Sleep.

Morning Routines

Have you ever noticed that cats and most animals stretch right after waking up? That's a good practice for us, too. Stretching improves your circulation and keeps you limber.

How about a big yawn and stretch? Taking several deep breaths will help to oxygenate your body. We need lots of oxygen and water.

Our bodies are about 70% water. Your brain is around 75% water. Start you day by drinking a big glass of water. Thinking clearly is difficult when you are dehydrated.

Next, it's a good practice to either read the Bible or other inspirational books. It starts your day on a positive and inspired mindset.

You may want to exercise in the morning, if time permits. Exercise should be an included activity in every day.

Then, go through your To-Do list again and visualize what you want to accomplish that day. When you have a clear picture in your head, it is more likely to happen.

Here are some suggested ideas to include in a typical morning routine.

Typical Morning Routine

- Alarm goes off at 6 AM or earlier.
- Stretch and take several deep breaths.
- Drink 2 cups of water. I usually add 1 TB Raw Apple Cider Vinegar.
- Spiritual devotions. Reading the Bible, or an inspirational book, and prayer.
- Exercise.
- Eat a healthy breakfast.
- Review your priorities.
- Start your day with the highest priority.

Start with the highest priority and work down the list. For me, the spiritual and physical goals are both done first thing in the morning. They are my top priorities.

Exercise, including walking, is a good way to get more oxygen in your body. You'll feel better too.

I like to mix in a bit more exercise through the day. I've got a rebounder and a number of health machines. It's easy to fit them in the day on breaks.

We only live this life once. Our health and activities today will determine how we will feel and be in our later years. One of my friends mentioned that her mother was already in a convalescent home in her 70's. Yet, I've seen videos of active Seniors accomplishing amazing feats in their 80's, 90's, and even an 104 year old man running in a race!

Here are some easy action items you may want to implement into your schedule:

Action Items

- Decide upon and write down your morning and evening routines. Include activities to help you get stronger both physically and spiritually.
- Write down the To-Dos you want to accomplish each day.
- See every day as a gift.
- End the day with personal reflection. What were you grateful for? How can you make tomorrow better?
- Write down your thoughts in a journal.

In the next chapter, we'll look at some ideas for helping your work to be more productive and organized. We'll also look at some time saving tips.

Organize Your Work

Here are some handy tips for getting more out of the time you work. These are ideas for office types of work. If you do not work in an office, there may still be a few ideas that are helpful for other tasks you might do.

Prioritize

This was mentioned under the evening routines, but is so important that it's worth repeating. One of my favorite stories about prioritizing took place over 100 years ago.

Charles Schwab, the president of Bethlehem Steel, was approached by Ivy Lee, an efficiency expert of that time. Here is the recorded verbal exchange between the two men.

Ivy Lee: "I can increase your people's efficiency – and your sales – if you will allow me to spend fifteen minutes with you."

Charles Schwab: "I need my people to take more action on projects. And, I don't have fifteen minutes to spend with you, I have about ten minutes as I'm going to be catching a train in fifteen minutes."

Ivy Lee: "Okay, that is fine! Take out a small piece of paper like the size of an index card, write down the five things you need to get taken care of right away."

Charles Schwab: "Uh, okay! Just write down the five, right?"

Ivy Lee: "Yes, that's correct. Now, mark off those in the order of importance that need to be accomplished immediately!"

Charles Schwab: "Okay, how much do I owe you for this?"

Ivy Lee: "If my idea works for you, then send me a check for whatever amount you think this idea was worth to you!"

Charles took Mr. Lee's advice and also told all of his executive to do the same. They were to make a list of the top 5 priorities and do them the next day.

At a time when people earned an average of $2 a day, Charles Schwab looked at their results and was so pleased that he sent a check to Ivy Lee for $25,000. They actually spent 25 minutes, so Mr. Lee earned $1000 a minute!

Pick your 4 or 5 top priorities and do them first. I heard this story many years ago, but it just stuck with me. I hope it encourages you, too. It's daunting to look at a long list of To-Dos. Pick the 4 or 5 most important ones and save the longer To-Do list if there is time.

My good friend Joyce Perkins says:

"Here is one of my mantras; prioritize EVERYTHING, tasks big and small, and "DO IT NOW". This keeps your life flowing and in order."
Joyce Perkins Co-founder and Former Executive Director, Los Angeles Neighborhood Initiative (LANI), Currently serving on the LANI Board of Directors

I like using the Inbox of Nozbe for the Brain Dump. Then, sort the ideas into the appropriate folders. To prioritize items, you just check the star and it shows up under the Priority Tab. Once there, it's easy to drag items to change the order.

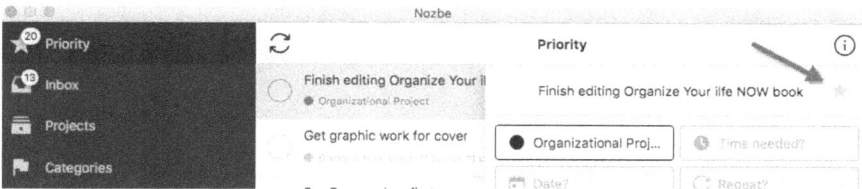

When you look at your list, are there items that someone else can do? Some things you will want to delete, others delegate, and then make decisions on the rest.

Mind Mapping

When you have your list of priorities. Using a mind map is terrific for expanding and brain storming on specific projects. Mind maps can range from simple to elaborate with pictures and many colors.

The main topic is in the center of the mind map. Branches are the various topic or ideas around the main theme and twigs are supporting ideas for each branch. Mind maps have a natural organizational structure that radiates from the central theme or project.

This kind of mapping has been used for years, but a British author, Tony Buzan, made it popular and coined the word 'mind map'. You can create mind maps by hand on paper or with a growing number of software applications.

A popular free mind map is called FreeMind. It has a simple but effective format. Here is a screenshot of a small portion of the beginning stages of writing this book. This is to give you an idea of what mind mapping looks like.

FreeMind is text based which makes it easy to add lots of explanatory text. The next image is from a popular online mind map program called Bubbl.us. They also have apps for mobile devices, like iPads. Since it is primarily web based, it is a good platform to use for sharing with others.

You may make 3 mind maps for free. Then, there is a monthly or yearly charge for unlimited mind maps. There is also an option to purchase multiple licenses for team members to use.

Here is a sample screen shot of Bubbl.us.

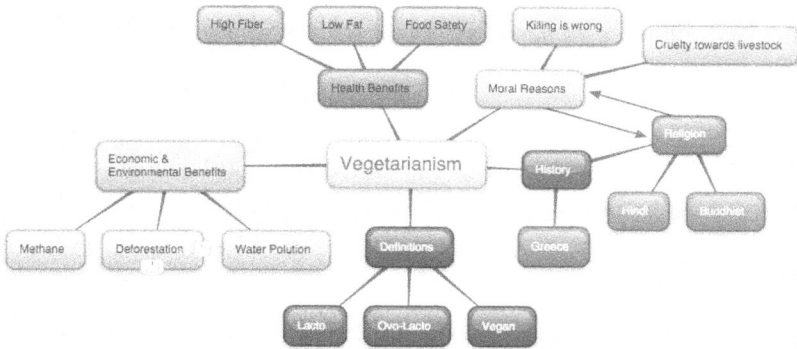

Can you see how this can be helpful? Using mind maps can help you organize your thoughts and can help you brainstorm different aspects of your projects.

Get all the ideas in your mind captured on paper or in a digital format. Then, you can take some of the bigger ideas and use mind mapping to help you brainstorm how to flesh out the steps for you ideas.

Mind maps are great for planning out vacations, studying, brainstorming new products, organizing work flows, and a myriad of projects.

Here is a screenshot of another program called Mind-nod Pro. It allows photos and images to be added to any of the text boxes as well as floating anywhere on the map.

This is a sample mind map I put together just to show you how it can look with photos or images.

Remember Important Dates

Having an organized life includes remembering items that need to get done on or by specific dates. With electronic calendars or a program like Nozbe, you can easily schedule repeating items.

For example, never forget the birthday of your family members and friends. Remember other important dates like anniversaries or holidays.

There are services for automatically sending out physical cards or e-cards. You can set these up in advance, or just use the reminder alerts to remember to make a phone call or lunch date, etc. People will be surprised at your great memory and will appreciate that they are special to you.

How about when your taxes are due? Being self-employed, I have to remember to pay quarterly sales tax. It's already set up in my system with a 2 week alert that pops up every quarter. I never need to worry about forgetting to pay taxes, business license fees, etc.

Ever buy something with a money-back guarantee? You can put the guarantee date in your calendar to decide if the product was helpful before the date expires. Set it up on the due date and schedule one or more alerts to remind you a few days before the guarantee is up.

All of these dates can be written each year into a physical calendar, at the beginning of the year. But, it is easiest to use an electronic option. Then, you only need to input the dates once to be automatically reminded every year.

Pomodoros

Have you heard of a pomodoro? It is a time management system started in the 1980's by Francesco Cirillo. He originally used a tomato shaped timer. Pomodoro is the Italian word for tomato. We work best when we are focused on one project at a time. The focus is in chunks of time with breaks. Here are the steps.

- Decide the task to focus on.
- Set the pomodoro timer to 20 - 25 minutes.
- Work on the task until the timer rings.
- Take a 5 minute break.
- After every 4 pomodoros, take a longer break, 10 to 20 minutes.

What I like about using pomodoros is the uninterrupted work periods and that it's a way to remember to keep standing up from the computer. Even if you get enough exercise, sitting for long periods will literally wipe out the benefits of exercising. Plus, it's better for your eyes to take a break from the screen at least every 20 minutes.

There are physical timers or computer programs that make it easy to keep track of the pomodoros. Just do a Google search and you can find them. During the short breaks, you can use a rebounder for a few minutes, get some water, or stretch. Also, focus your eyes on a distant object for a few seconds.

Work on one task at a time. If you are on the computer, shut down your email software, Skype, and any browser tabs that you are not using. It's easier to focus without being drawn away by incoming email or open windows.

This is also why having an uncluttered work space is important. It's easier to focus without other To-Do items in sight. Your computer also runs faster without extra programs open and running in the background.

Email Strategies

You might want to consider moving your email to Gmail. They have a very good spam filter that will make it easier to stop unwanted emails from even hitting your Inbox.

Constantly checking your email can waste a lot of time. Instead of leaving your email software open, try checking only a few times per day. Just give yourself 5 or 10 minutes to see if there is anything important that you want to respond to.

You can use a free service called 'unroll.me' to unsubscribe from subscription emails you no longer want to see, and you can see all of your subscriptions in one place.

They send you one email a day with all of the subscriptions listed. Then, you have the option to read more of any message that looks interesting. When you click it, you'll see the entire email and have the option to unsubscribe, too.

Make decisions now. If there is an email that needs a quick response, do it now. Only archive emails you may want to reference later, like receipts for purchases or business correspondents.

If it's an email that you need to answer or want to spend time with later, and it'll take over 2 minutes, either put it in a special folder or forward it to your organizational platform, like Nozbe.

Most services will let you set up folders or labels to be applied automatically to incoming emails. You can tag important people in your life to be sent to a smart folder, so you don't miss their messages. In Mac Mail, you right click on a name and add contacts to the VIP list. Then they show up in a folder separate from the regular InBox.

I have also used services like 'Spam Arrest' which dramatically cut down your spam emails. This is a good idea if you are not using an online service like Gmail.

Have you heard the term Inbox Zero? It takes great discipline to make upfront decisions on every email that is in your Inbox. Inbox Zero is when you process your email to zero every time you check your Inbox.

Most of the emails should probably be deleted. The rest you can archive, act on, or forward to a place for taking action later.

If it's an email I want to read later, I send it to Evernote via a special email that is assigned to my account. Evernote has notebooks and tags. Emails go into the default notebook, but you can also specify which notebook the email goes to by adding @[notebook name] in the subject line, or tag it with #[tag name].

If it's an email that requires an action and takes longer than 2 minutes, I forward it to my Nozbe Inbox by a special email from that account. Both Things and OmniFocus have this capability as well.

Once you have forwarded the emails, it's a good idea to archive them just in case you need to look them up again and as a precaution if one of the other online services goes down.

Most email services also provide the option to make email rules. If you notice a particular type of spam email that's getting through the filters, set it up to automatically delete.

Track Your Time

To see how you are using your time, there is an excellent online free timer called Toggl. In time management programs I've read, they always recommend keeping track of your time for at least a week to see how it's spent.

Toggl makes this easy. You start a timer when you begin a new activity. Then, when you change activities, stop the timer. Log what you're doing, and start a new timer.

It also has apps for windows, OS X, and Linux so you can use it wherever you are. You can track activities everywhere. This app is especially good for those in a business that are paid by time. Plus, it's good for anyone to get an idea of how their time is actually spent.

You could use paper to track your time by jotting down, every 15 minutes, what you have done. I've used that system in the past and prefer Toggl.

They have a Chrome extension to make it even easier to keep track of your time. Included is the option to trigger pomodoros which is a very nice addition.

Tracking your time can be a real eye opener. It can help to get you refocused. It's something that I do periodically, but not as an ongoing everyday activity.

Background Music

Several studies have come out about the benefits of studying with background music. In particular, baroque music or music by Mozart seems to help people focus. More of our brains are active when listening to good music. They are most active when playing an instrument, but listening can help you focus, too.

One of the studies was by David Merrell. He won the Virginia State Science Fair in the late 1990's. He used 72 mice split into 3 groups. He used a standard maze and tested each group before introducing them to music. They all took around 10 minutes to get through the maze.

One group heard Mozart for 12 hours a day, another silence, and the third heard a heavy metal group for 12 hours a day. After a few weeks the classical music group got through the maze in 1 1/2 minutes, the no music group took around 5 minutes and the heavy metal group took half an hour.

They, the heavy metal group, also became very aggressive and started killing each other!

Other studies show how music actually effects the way brain cells grow. Listening to good music has been proven to reduce blood pressure, your heart rate, and reduce the hormones related to stress.

In my Amazon Prime account, I've set up Classical Music to Study by. I find it easier to concentrate with music without words. It makes working even more fun.

You can also find instrumental classical study music on YouTube. I particularly like the 'Bach To Work' music, although the ads are distracting.

As a bonus idea, playing a musical instrument has been shown to be even more beneficial than just listening to music. Playing music uses both hemispheres of your brain. It's fun and can be started at any age.

Here are a few action items from this chapter.

Action Items

- Always prioritize your list with the most important items first.
- Try using pomodoros and see if it's beneficial for you.
- Check your emails just 2 or 3 times a day, unless you need to do more for your work.
- Quickly process each email until your Inbox is empty.
- Track your time for a week to assess how you are spending it.
- Consider listening to instrumental music.
- Bonus: Think about learning to play an instrument. It's so wonderful for your brain and overall health!

In the next chapter, we'll look at some of the main action steps summarized. I also suggest reading through this book again with a highlighter, pen, and paper. Then, when you see an idea that you want to implement, highlight it, and write down specifically

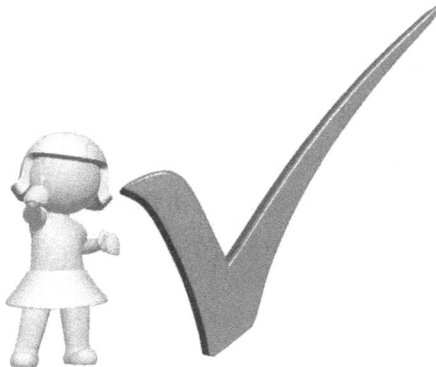

Action Steps

We've looked at why it's important to get organized. It saves you time, energy, and money. You've now gotten some ideas how to free up your thoughts, your surroundings, and have ideas of what tools can help. There have been action ideas throughout the book. Here are the main ones to concentrate on for an organized life.

1. Life Goals

The best place to start is by getting your thinking uncluttered. Set aside a couple hours to look at the goals that are most important to you. Make your goals specific and measurable.

For example, if you have a goal of drinking 8 cups of water a day. Fill 2 quart containers with water and drink it throughout the day. You'll know you've met your goal when the containers are empty.

2. Brain Dump

Next, do a Brain Dump and capture all those thoughts on paper, or in a program like Nozbe. What's great about this is that you can continue to add your thoughts to your system and nothing is lost.

When I'm working through a pomodoro and something pops

into my mind that I want to remember, I immediately add it to Nozbe with a few clicks of the mouse. To easily add To-Dos, I leave Nozbe open in the background. This helps me to refocus back on the project knowing the thought is captured.

Then, when your mind is clear and with your life goals in mind, that's the best time to go conquer the surrounding clutter.

Brain Dumps should be an ongoing activity. In your evening review, it is a good time to see if there are any more ideas or thoughts you want to capture.

3. Set Up Your System

Set up a system so you can easily retrieve anything you own. In this book, I've suggested using a program like FileMaker. Decide on your 'storage' places. A file cabinet with hanging folders works great for papers, but you can also designate desk drawers, book shelves, and any type of storage area.

For the cabinet with hanging folders, you can number the folder starting with #1. Put a tab on the hanging folder with the number '1'. Each folder can hold as many papers as you want. I like to keep it to around 12. Put the paper in your folder and notate it in the software. Include several words in the description that can help you find the it later.

If you are not sure how to set up a database or you prefer to use a dedicated solution for filing your stuff, there is an easy solution called Paper Tiger. It works both in the Cloud and on PCs.

If you want to store everything in the Cloud, you can scan physical papers into the computer to make them digitally accessible. This is also an excellent solution for businesses to store and share files via the Internet. Evernote can read the text of scanned papers and PDF files. This makes them easy to find and accessible from any location.

4. Use Your System

Start with the most visible clutter first. Toss, act on, or keep everything you touch. If it's something you want to act on later, put it in your InBox paper tray. If there is a due date, schedule it in your calendar so it's not forgotten.

Once the visible clutter is gone, tackle the hidden clutter, like drawers, closets, etc. Get your system set up and when anything new comes through the door, make a decision to act on it now. Don't let papers stack up.

Getting a system up and running can take quite a bit of time. But, once it's in place and you're using it, it's worth it. Once your system is set up, it is quite easy to maintain and will save you a ton of time in the long run.

If you are not a computer person, an alternative is to decide where you will put all of your items and write it down in a notebook. For example, all the manuals could be in a folder in your file cabinets labeled 'Manuals'.

When you buy anything with a manual, always paper clip the receipt inside the front cover of the manual and store it in your system. Then, if the device needs to be repaired years later, you will have the proof of purchase easily accessible right inside the front cover of the Instructional manual.

5. Be Aware Of Your Thoughts and Body Language

Healthy thoughts can change your brain. Be aware of your thoughts and your posture. It has been discovered that your body language can actually change how you feel and how you are perceived.

A quick tip for good posture is to stand against a wall with your head and shoulders touching the wall. Then, walk away and try to keep that basic position. Another quick tip is to imagine a string is tied to the top of your head, pulling it towards the ceiling.

Harvard Business School professor Amy Cuddy shared her research findings on how our body language can change how other perceive us. Even our own body chemistry is changed by our posture. People's hormones actually changed after a few minutes of better posture. She shared her findings in a TED Talk a few years ago.

6. Review

I suggest reading through this book a few more times and highlight or take notes on the things that you want to implement now.

With these simple steps you can think more clearly, focus, and get more done. Your life is so special. It's my hope that some of the ideas in this book can help you to live it to the fullest!

We are just here for a short time. And, each of us have something unique to share with the world.

It's amazing that there are no two people with the same finger prints. We each have a unique voice and I believe we also each have a special purpose in this life.

As the Good Book says, it's in serving others that we are most blessed! Wishing you a joyous journey in your life on earth.

God Bless you!

The final chapter has a list of helpful resources. For the most up to date list visit:

GraciousPublishing.com/resources

Resources

Several resources and tools were mentioned in this book. Here are some of the additional resources you may find helpful in organizing your life.

Books & Videos

Getting Things Done - Robert Allen

Good book for learning more details on how to think about prioritizing, and more tips on getting things done.

OfferLast.com/done

7 Laws Of A Learner - Bruce Wilkinson

Excellent book on how to teach, but also on encouraging the people around you. It includes many specific examples.

OfferLast.com/learner

The Miracle Morning: The Not-So-Obvious Secret Guaranteed to Transform Your Life (Before 8AM)

What do most successful people have in common? They get up early. This is an excellent book with tips on how to become an early morning riser.

OfferLast.com/morning

The 12 Week Year: Get More Done in 12 Weeks than Others Do in 12 Months

An interesting way to think about goals. It's easier to envision getting something finished in 3 months instead of focusing on one year goals.

OfferLast.com/12weeks

Personal Prayer Journal - Jean Welles

Good place to record and track your prayers. I've used several prayer journals but none were set up the way I like to pray, so I made one that does.

GraciousPublishing.com/prayer-journal

Worship Guitar Class - Jean Welles

This is my guitar website. This is where you can learn to play the guitar effortlessly with excellent technique.

WorshipGuitarClass.com

Software Tools & Services

Nozbe

This is the software tool that I'm using every day to organize my tasks. It's assessable as an app on any device and in web browsers. You can also use it as a place to communicate with team members. It integrates seamlessly with programs like Evernote and DropBox. For a 10% discount, use the code 'special'.

OfferLast.com/nozbe

OmniFocus

This is a full feature Mac only software tool. It is an excellent tool I used to use.

OfferLast.com/omnifocus

Things

Only for Macs. A program I used to use for capturing ideas and planning the activities for each day.

OfferLast.com/things

Trello

A free tool for planning out projects. Works on any type of computer or smart phone and you can share the boards with others.

OfferLast.com/trello

Paper Tiger

Excellent alternative to using FileMaker. Can be a software program on your PC or hosted in the Cloud for sharing with others.

OfferLast.com/papertiger

Manage WP

If you have Wordpress websites, this service will save you a lot of time. You can manage and update everything from one dashboard. With a click of a button all of your plug-ins on any server will be updated.

OfferLast.com/manage

DropBox

Extremely useful service for sharing and storing large files over several platforms. You can specify which folder or items to share with other or keep them private. You can start with 2 Gigs of space free.

OfferLast.com/dropbox

Evernote

Easy way to collect and find notes, images, and more. It syncs over all your devices. It's free, but also has paid options for more storage and capabilities.

OfferLast.com/evernote

Last Pass

Neat solution to safely storing passwords. It's free for your local computer and there is a small yearly charge to access passwords from your mobile devices. There is also an Enterprise option for storing and sharing passwords with groups of people.

OfferLast.com/lastpass

1Password

Another solution for safely storing passwords. This is a good solution for families or individuals. It's a one time fee and you can sync all of your devices. They have the option of sharing passwords with team members.

OfferLast.com/1password

Stretch-It-Out-Strap

Excellent strap for stretching by Geri Gates
OfferLast.com/strap

Check out the website for more items to help you organize your life: Updated resources.:

GraciousPublishing.com/resources

50 Clever Organizational Tips

Want more tips? Download '50 Clever Organizational Tips' at **GraciousPublishing.com/50tips**

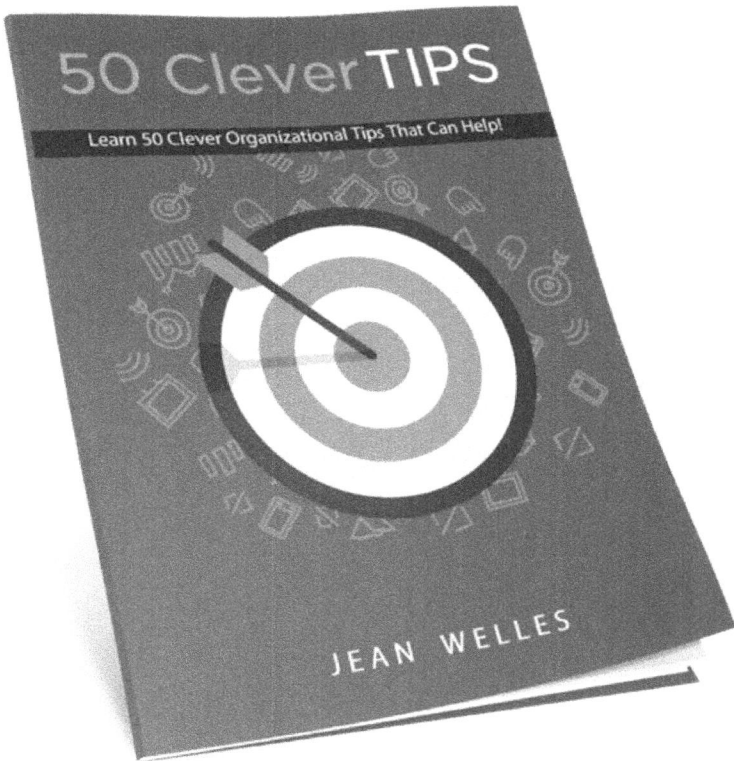